LET'S
see

Passover

by Natalie M. Rosinsky

Content Adviser: Ina Regosin, Dean of Students, Hebrew College,
Newton Centre, Massachusetts

Reading Adviser: Rosemary G. Palmer, Ph.D.,
Department of Literacy, College of Education,
Boise State University

Let's See Library
Compass Point Books
Minneapolis, Minnesota

Compass Point Books
3109 West 50th Street, #115
Minneapolis, MN 55410

Visit Compass Point Books on the Internet at *www.compasspointbooks.com*
or e-mail your request to *custserv@compasspointbooks.com*

On the cover: A seder plate

Photographs ©: Photodisc, cover; Roger Ressmeyer/Corbis, 4, 12; Hulton/Archive by Getty Images, 6;
Stock Montage, Inc., 8; Reuters/Reinhard Krause/Corbis, 10; Arthur Gurmankin, Mary Morina/Unicorn Stock Photos, 14;
Eric Schwab/AFP/Getty Images, 16; Shelley Gazin/Corbis, 18; Annie Griffiths Belt/Corbis, 20.

Creative Director: Terri Foley
Managing Editor: Catherine Neitge
Photo Researcher: Marcie C. Spence
Designers: Melissa Kes and Les Tranby
Educational Consultant: Diane Smolinski

Library of Congress Cataloging-in-Publication Data
Rosinsky, Natalie M. (Natalie Myra)
   Passover / Natalie M. Rosinsky.
      p. cm. — (Let's see)
   Includes index.
ISBN 0-7565-0772-3 (hardcover)
1. Passover—Juvenile literature. I. Title. II. Series.
BM695.P3R673 2004
296.4'37—dc22   2004005020

Table of Contents

NOTE: In this book, words that are defined in the glossary
*are in **bold** the first time they appear in the text.*

What Is Passover?

A special meal, a story about freedom, and family are important during the Jewish holiday of Passover.

Jews remember their escape long ago from slavery. They **celebrate** being free. They may remember other dangers they have faced. Jews also think about the struggles of people everywhere to be free.

Passover lasts seven or eight days depending on where you live. It takes place every spring. The dates each year depend on the Jewish calendar.

◄ *Jewish boys wear skullcaps called yarmulkes (pronounced YAH-mi-kuhs) during Passover.*

6

What Is the Story of Passover?

More than 3,000 years ago, Jews were slaves in Egypt. They suffered under the Egyptians. A man named Moses became their leader. He asked the Egyptian king, or Pharaoh, to free the Jews. Pharaoh refused.

Jews believe that God then helped them by sending 10 terrible **plagues.** Now the Egyptians suffered. The last plague was the death of first-born sons. To escape this one, the Jews painted their doorways with lambs' blood. This sign told the spirit of death to "pass over" those houses.

Pharaoh was frightened. He freed the Jews. They fled out of Egypt in a great hurry. They feared Pharaoh might change his mind!

◄ Moses raises his rod as one of the plagues—a huge storm with hail—hits Egypt.

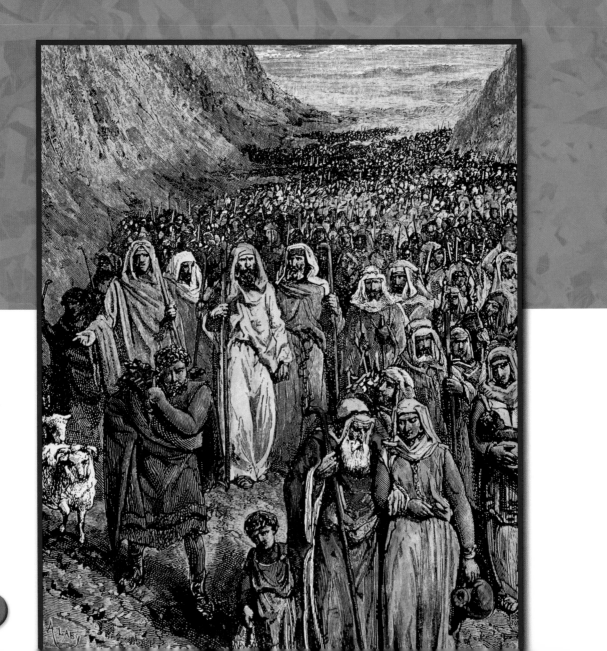

How Was Passover First Observed?

The Jews reached the land that is now Israel. Moses told them always to remember their springtime escape. They thanked God. They honored the **miracles** that had saved them. Because death "passed over" their houses, the Jews called this holiday Passover.

They prepared foods their grandparents had eaten as they fled Egypt. At this feast, Jews told the story of this hasty escape.

Over time, some Jews in different communities forgot about Passover. Jewish leaders called rabbis then wrote rules for this holiday.

◄ *Moses leads the Jews out of Egypt and into Israel.*

What Are Ways Passover Is Observed?

Because Jews hurried from Egypt, their bread did not have time to rise. They carried flat, **unleavened** bread with them. During Passover, Jews eat special unleavened bread called matzoh. They do not eat foods that contain **leavening.** Before Passover, they remove all such foods from their homes.

The night before Passover, children enjoy searching for tiny pieces of bread. The crumbs are swept into a bag and disposed of.

On the first two nights of Passover, Jewish families gather together. They have a special meal called a seder (pronounced SAY-der). During this meal, they tell the story of Passover.

◄ *An Israeli man and other Orthodox Jews pray and burn bread containing leavening in a ritual fire before the start of Passover.*

What Is Served at the Passover Seder?

Special foods are served at the seder. Some of them are **symbols** of the Passover story. They are put on a decorated seder plate. As the story is told, the speaker points to each food.

The bitter root, called horseradish, represents the bitterness of slavery. A mix of chopped fruit and nuts stands for the clay that slaves used to make bricks. A green vegetable stands for the joy of springtime and being free.

Matzoh rests on a separate plate. It represents the hurried escape from Egypt.

◄ *A rabbi explains the meaning of the special foods served during Passover.*

FRANCE
PASSOVER HAGGADAH
THE MIXING OF FOODS
Blessed are You, Lord our God, Ruler of the universe,
Who sanctified us with His commandments, and com-
manded us to observe the Eruv.
With this Eruv it shall be permissible for us to bake, cook,
keep food warm, light the candles, and make all necessary
preparations on the festival for the Sabbath. This shall be
permitted for us and for all Jews who live in this city.
LIGHTING THE FESTIVAL CANDLES
ערוב תבשילין
THE MIXING OF FOODS
THE PREPARATION OF THE SEDER TABLE

What Happens at the Passover Seder?

Each person reads or listens to the Passover story. It is written partly in **Hebrew** in a decorated book called a Haggadah (pronounced ha-GAH-dah). People sit in comfort to listen. They are reminded that slaves were not allowed to rest this way.

People drink wine or grape juice. A cup is left for the **prophet** Elijah. They hope another miracle will bring his arrival.

The youngest child always asks four important questions. To end the seder, children hunt for a hidden piece of matzoh called the afikomen (pronounced ah-fee-KO-men). The finder gets a prize!

◄ *The Haggadah has short prayers in Hebrew and Passover songs to sing.*

How Has Passover Changed?

Over the years, the Haggadah has changed. Today, the written Passover story often includes other dangers Jews have faced.

These include the terrible experiences of Jews during World War II (1939–1945). Millions of European Jews and others were murdered by the Nazi government in Germany. This is called the Holocaust. At a seder, Jews sometimes honor and pray for other people who still struggle to be free.

Jews continue to create new Passover **customs.** In the 1970s, some people began adding a special cup for Miriam at their seder table. Miriam was the sister of Moses. She helped lead the Jews from Egypt.

◄ *Survivors of Buchenwald, a Nazi concentration camp in Germany, were freed at the end of the war in 1945. Thousands of people were killed at this prison camp.*

How Is Passover Observed in the United States?

Passover is not a national holiday in the United States. Government offices, schools, and businesses are open during Passover. Some Jews, though, do not work or go to school on the first two days of this holiday. Some Jews also do not work on the last two days.

Many Jewish families enjoy a **tradition** of gathering for each seder. It is a custom to invite guests. Often, these are other Jews whose families are far away. Sometimes, guests are friends or neighbors who are not Jewish.

◄ *A family enjoys a seder during Passover.*

How Is Passover Observed Around the World?

In Israel, Passover is observed for seven days. The first and last days are national holidays. Schools, government offices, and businesses are closed then. Some Jews work only half days during the rest of Passover.

Around the world, Jews have different seder traditions. In Spain, Egypt, India, Iraq, and Syria, people act out the Passover story. They carry sacks of matzoh and pretend they are escaping slavery.

Wherever Passover is observed, it is a time to remember and tell the story of the Jewish people's journey from slavery to freedom.

◄ *Family members celebrate Passover with a picnic in Jerusalem, Israel.*

Glossary

celebrate—to enjoy and honor something
customs—a group of people's usual way of doing things
Hebrew—the language Jews speak in Israel and all Jews use in prayers
leavening—the part of bread dough that makes it rise
miracles—acts that people believe are caused by God

plagues—terrible illnesses or events
prophet—someone who speaks or acts for God
symbols—things that represent other things
tradition—a group of people's longtime way of doing things
unleavened—lacking the part of bread dough that makes it rise

Did You Know?

✱ God sent nine plagues before the one that called for the death of first-born sons. They were blood, frogs, lice, wild beasts, cattle disease, boils, hail, locusts, and darkness.

✱ The rules for Passover were set near Israel. Rabbis there knew when people would see the new moon. They would always begin the holiday on the right day. This is why Passover is celebrated for only seven days in Israel. It lasts eight days everywhere else in the world because the rabbis knew the new moon appears later in far away places.

✱ Here are the four questions plus an introductory question that the youngest child asks on Passover: Why is this night different from all other nights?
1. Why is it that on all other nights during the year we eat either bread or matzoh, but on this night we eat matzoh?
2. Why is it that on all other nights we eat all kinds of vegetables, but on this night we eat bitter herbs?
3. Why is it on all other nights we do not dip even once, but on this night we dip twice?
4. Why is it that on all other nights we eat either sitting or reclining, but on this night we eat in a reclining position?

Want to Know More?

At the Library

Fisher, Leonard Everett. *Moses: Retold from the Bible.* New York: Holiday House, 1995.

Hoyt-Goldsmith, Diane. *Celebrating Passover.* New York: Holiday House, 2000.

Manushkin, Fran. *Miriam's Cup: A Passover Story.* New York: Scholastic, 1998.

On the Web

For more information on *Passover,* use FactHound to track down Web sites related to this book.

1. Go to *www.facthound.com*
2. Type in a search word related to this book or this book ID: 0756507723.
3. Click on the *Fetch It* button.

Your trusty FactHound will fetch the best Web sites for you!

On the Road

The Jewish Museum
1109 Fifth Ave.
New York, NY 10128
212/423-3200
To visit an art museum that explores Jewish culture

Spertus Museum
of the Spertus Institute of Jewish Studies
618 S. Michigan Ave.
Chicago, IL 60605
312/322-1747
To see old and new seder plates, Elijah's and Miriam's cups, and Haggadoth from around the world

National Museum of Jewish American History
55 N. Fifth St.
Philadelphia, PA 19106
215/923-3811
To find out more about Jews and Jewish holidays in the United States

Index

About the Author

Natalie M. Rosinsky writes about history, social studies, economics, science, and other fun things. One of her two cats usually sits on her computer as she works in Mankato, Minnesota. Natalie earned graduate degrees from the University of Wisconsin and has been a high school and college teacher.